FAMOUS LIVES

The Story of
SHIRLEY TEMPLE BLACK
Hollywood's Youngest Star

FAMOUS LIVES
titles in Large-Print Editions:

The Story of Louisa May Alcott: Determined Writer

The Story of Muhammad Ali:
  Heavyweight Champion of the World

The Story of Alexander Graham Bell: Inventor of the Telephone

The Story of Shirley Temple Black: Hollywood's Youngest Star

The Story of George Bush:
  The Forty-first President of the United States

The Story of Roberto Clemente: All-Star Hero

The Story of Bill Clinton and Al Gore: Our Nation's Leaders

The Story of Hillary Rodham Clinton:
  First Lady of the United States

The Story of Christopher Columbus: Admiral of the Ocean Sea

The Story of Davy Crockett: Frontier Hero

The Story of Walt Disney: Maker of Magical Worlds

The Story of Frederick Douglass: Voice of Freedom

The Story of Benjamin Franklin: Amazing American

The Story of Jim Henson: Creator of the Muppets

The Story of Martin Luther King, Jr.: Marching to Freedom

The Story of Abraham Lincoln: President for the People

The Story of Thurgood Marshall: Justice for All

The Story of Pocahontas: Indian Princess

The Story of Colin Powell and Benjamin O. Davis, Jr.:
  Two American Generals

The Story of Jackie Robinson: Bravest Man in Baseball

The Story of Babe Ruth: Baseball's Greatest Legend

The Story of Sacajawea: Guide to Lewis and Clark

The Story of Junípero Serra: Brave Adventurer

The Story of Sitting Bull: Great Sioux Chief

The Story of Annie Sullivan: Helen Keller's Teacher

The Story of Squanto: First Friend to the Pilgrims

The Story of Harriet Tubman:
  Conductor of the Underground Railroad

The Story of George Washington: Quiet Hero

The Story of Laura Ingalls Wilder: Pioneer Girl

The Story of Malcolm X: Civil Rights Leader

FAMOUS LIVES

The Story of
SHIRLEY TEMPLE BLACK
Hollywood's Youngest Star

By Carlo Fiori

Gareth Stevens Publishing
MILWAUKEE

Dedicated to Kate and Daryl Eisenbart

For a free color catalog describing Gareth Stevens Publishing's list of high-quality books and multimedia programs, call 1-800-542-2595 (USA) or 1-800-461-9120 (Canada). Gareth Stevens Publishing's Fax: (414) 225-0377.
See our catalog, too, on the World Wide Web: http://gsinc.com

Library of Congress Cataloging-in-Publication Data

Fiori, Carlo.
    The story of Shirley Temple Black: Hollywood's youngest star / by Carlo Fiori.
      p. cm. — (Famous lives)
    Originally published: New York: Dell, © 1990, in series: Dell yearling biography.
    Filmography: pp. 95-97.
    Includes index.
    Summary: A biography of the popular child actress who grew up to have many interesting careers as an adult, including that of businesswoman, author, and diplomat.
    ISBN 0-8368-1481-9 (lib. bdg.)
    1. Temple, Shirley, 1928- —Juvenile literature. 2. Motion picture actors and actresses—United States—Biography—Juvenile literature. 3. Ambassadors—United States—Biography—Juvenile literature. [1. Temple, Shirley, 1928- . 2. Actors and actresses. 3. Women—Biography.] I. Title. II. Series: Famous lives (Milwaukee, Wis.)
PN2287.T33F56 1997
791.43'028'092—dc21
    [B]   97-1054

The events described in this book are true. They have been carefully researched and excerpted from authentic biographies, writings, and commentaries. No part of this biography has been fictionalized. To learn more about Shirley Temple Black, refer to the list of books and videos at the back of this book, or ask your librarian to recommend other fine books and videos.

First published in this edition in North America in 1997 by
Gareth Stevens Publishing
1555 North RiverCenter Drive, Suite 201
Milwaukee, Wisconsin 53212 USA

Original © 1990 by Parachute Press, Inc., as a Yearling Biography. Published by arrangement with Bantam Doubleday Dell Books for Young Readers, a division of Bantam Doubleday Dell Publishing Group, Inc. Additional end matter © 1997 by Gareth Stevens, Inc.

The trademark Yearling® is registered in the U.S. Patent and Trademark Office.
The trademark Dell® is registered in the U.S. Patent and Trademark Office.

Printed in the United States of America

1 2 3 4 5 6 7 8 9 01 00 99 98 97

Contents

Introduction

"Sparkle!" her nervous mother urged as little Shirley Temple raced out onto the brightly lit movie set.

The other actors looked at the bouncy blonde suspiciously. They couldn't understand why the studio had hired this five year old to be in a movie for grown-ups.

But Shirley didn't pay any attention to them. She could hardly wait to begin her act. All week, she had practiced the words to her song. She had even added her own steps to the tap dance. Now, when the music started, she fluffed up her new polka-dotted dress and began singing and dancing.

Shirley's mother, Gertrude, breathed a sigh of

relief. The other actors perked up. Everyone could see that this curly-headed little girl was very talented. Her spirit of fun was catching, and soon everyone on the set was smiling.

Later that night, when the head of the movie company saw the scene on film, he couldn't believe his eyes. The child was terrific! Immediately, he ordered his writers to create more scenes for Shirley. He also convinced her parents to sign a contract hiring Shirley for the next seven years!

No one knew then that Shirley Temple would soon be the most popular movie star in the world. But that's just what happened.

When Shirley made her movie debut in 1931, people all across the country were hungry and frightened. It was the time of the Great Depression, a period when jobs and food were hard to find. So it wasn't surprising that Americans everywhere turned to the movies to forget their troubles.

Though they had no way of knowing when the hard times would finally end, watching Shirley made people laugh and feel happy—if only for one night. Even the President, Franklin Delano Roosevelt, was a Shirley Temple fan. "It is a splendid thing that for just fifteen cents an American can go to a movie and look at the smiling face of a baby and forget his troubles," he said.

Out of nowhere, it seemed, this perky little girl became famous! The actors and directors she worked with called her a "natural." As far as they could tell, singing and dancing and being a star were as easy as 1, 2, 3 for Shirley.

The truth, however, was somewhat different.

The story of little Shirley's sudden discovery is in fact a story of years of hard work and daily practice. It is the story of a mother's dream and of a young girl who delighted in making that dream come true.

Shirley's love of work and her love of people carried her through many interesting careers long after she gave up acting, including that of a businesswoman, author, and diplomat. Her life has been dedicated to helping others, and she isn't through yet. A grandmother now, Shirley Temple still believes in testing herself every day.

And it all began when she was just a baby in her crib. . . .

Starting Out

Looking down at baby Shirley, Gertrude Temple was so happy she could cry. Her two sons were almost teenagers, and she had practically given up hope of ever having a baby girl. But on April 23, 1928, Shirley was born.

Even strangers remarked that this cuddly, cheerful infant was truly special. When Gertrude played songs on the record player or sang to herself, Shirley seemed to listen. She would stand up in her crib, swaying in time with the music. When she took her first steps at one year old, she stood on her toes like a dancer.

Gertrude and her husband George, a banker, lived with their three children in a bright, sunny,

Spanish-style house in Santa Monica, a seaside community near Los Angeles, California. Palm trees waved in the gentle ocean breeze and brightly colored flowers bloomed all year in the mild climate. It was a pleasant life. But Gertrude wanted more than a pleasant life. She wanted a glamorous one. As a young girl herself, she had wanted to be an actress or a dancer. Now she wanted the same thing for Shirley. And this time she was determined to make it happen!

By the time Shirley was born, Americans had fallen in love with the movies, and movie producers were always looking for new and unusual talent. Like many other mothers of bright little girls, Gertrude read about such stars as Baby Peggy, who had earned one million dollars in just one year! And Gertrude just *knew* Shirley could be as famous.

At age three, Shirley started dance lessons. Each day, she practiced her dance steps over and over again. She loved every minute of her lessons, and she learned all kinds of dances. She studied tap, soft-shoe, ballroom, clog, and ballet.

One day, when Shirley was three-and-a-half years old, about two hundred children gathered at her dance school to audition for a movie series called *Baby Burlesks*. Shirley tried out and then immediately hid under the piano because she disliked one of the men in charge. But it didn't matter. She was chosen anyway.

Acting in these movies turned out to be an unusual job. In each film, Shirley had to imitate a different famous movie star while a group of young boys acted as her admirers. Part of what was supposed to make this movie funny was the costumes. From the waist up, all the children were dressed as adults. But on the bottom, they wore diapers!

Gertrude was thrilled that Shirley had gotten the part until she found out that the producer had lied to her. It turned out that Shirley and the other young actors had to rehearse long hours for free. And when the films were complete, they were paid very low wages. The Temples had trusted the Hollywood executives to treat Shirley fairly. Maybe they were *too* trusting.

Still, *Baby Burlesks* introduced the excited young Shirley to moviemaking. She quickly learned to understand such technical phrases as "put the baby in the fireplace." That means that the lighting director should focus a small spotlight on a scene. And when the director told her to "hit the marks," she knew he wanted her to move to the proper place on the set by noting the chalk marks on the floor out of the corner of her eye—without obviously peeking. Unfortunately, Shirley was too short to "hit the marks." But she came up with her own method. In rehearsals, she could figure out exactly where to stand by noticing which areas of her face were being warmed by the big, hot movie lights. Clearly, even as a young child, Shirley was an independent problem-solver!

Working long hours under hot lights, Shirley soon found out that moviemaking can be very tiring and even dangerous. In one scene, Shirley had to be hit by clods of dirt. In another, she had to be accidentally knocked to the floor. Once she had to ride in a cart pulled by an ostrich! Unfortunately, the ostrich panicked and threw Shirley to the ground.

Why didn't Shirley's mother object to these kinds of dangers? Because she didn't even know about them! The *Baby Burlesks* moviemakers kept all family members away from the set during filming. A child welfare worker who came to check the working conditions on the set was actually lured into a dressing room and "accidentally" locked inside!

Because no caring adults were allowed to watch out for the children, the moviemakers got away with using a cruel punishment. When Shirley (or any of the other children) wasted time or misbehaved on the set, she was locked in a dark, hot box with a block of ice. The heat would make Shirley feel weak, but she couldn't sit down because the water from the melting ice block covered the floor. Unfortunately, Shirley was almost as stubborn as she was talented. She was sent to that box more than once. Even so, she remained the star of eight of the *Baby Burlesks*.

Gertrude Temple had a lot to do with Shirley's success. When Gertrude was a girl, she had loved to read stories aloud, acting out all the parts. And when she became a mother, she always read to all her children. But now that her sons were older, she could really concentrate on Shirley. Every night, as if it were a game, Gertrude would read the script to Shirley and explain what the next day's filming was all about. She would help Shirley understand how her character was supposed to feel. Did the script call for her to act sad? Funny? Serious?

Shirley and her mother enjoyed preparing for the next day's activities this way. They shared the fun of make-believe, and, to this day, Shirley is grateful for her mother's patience and cleverness.

Shirley's movie career was off to a good start. But then, in 1933, when Shirley was just five years old, the movie producer who had hired her went bankrupt. He had no more money to make new films, and no other producer wanted to hire Shirley. After only about a year and a half in the movies, Shirley was out of work! All of her mother's hopes and plans suddenly seemed to fall apart.

But almost as suddenly, Shirley was back in business. One night, she was dancing playfully on the sidewalk outside a theater that was showing one of her short films, when a songwriter from New York City passed by. He recognized her immediately and was happy to hear that she wanted to make more movies.

Just a few days later, Shirley was invited to the world-famous Fox film studio to audition for a new movie called *Stand Up and Cheer*. It had a song-and-dance number called "Baby Take a Bow" that the New York songwriter thought Shirley would be perfect for! A young girl had already been chosen for it, but many of the people working on the movie didn't think she was very good.

When Shirley tried out, everyone agreed that she was just right! The part was hers! But the fun *and* the work were just beginning.

The musical scenes for *Stand Up and Cheer* were filmed in a very complicated way. First, the performers had to make a recording of the sound: the talking, singing, and tap dance rhythms. Next, all the action had to be filmed in time with the recording.

During the filming, the actors only *pretended* to sing because they had already recorded the song. This technique, called "pantomime," was harder than it looked. Shirley and the other actors had to move their lips to match the words on the recording *exactly* and, at the same time, move their feet *exactly* with the recorded tapping! This was very hard for most actors to do, and it was often necessary to shoot such scenes over and over again. But Shirley, to everyone's surprise, was always perfectly "in sync," or matched, throughout the filming!

Gertrude was happy that Shirley was making movies again. And the Fox executives were happy to have Shirley working for them!

Writers were immediately told to find old movie scripts or to write new ones that would show off Shirley's talents. Newspaper and magazine reporters came to interview the young star. Costume designers, set designers, directors, and cameramen all did their part to present Shirley to the public.

The studio announced Shirley's age as four years old, although she was really five. They thought people would like her *more* if they thought she was younger. Shirley didn't learn her real age until her twelfth—which actually turned out to be her *thirteenth*—birthday party!

Shirley, of course, was too young to understand what all this special treatment meant. And Gertrude was determined to keep her from being spoiled. Still, trying to raise Shirley Temple as if she were just *any* little girl would soon become a very *big* job!

Fame

Gertrude knew that movie fame could be good *and* bad. Other child stars had been famous for a short time, and were then quickly forgotten. Stardom sometimes ruined friendships and families. One of the most famous child actors of the time had taken his parents to court because they spent every cent of the four million dollars he had earned, leaving him nothing.

Many fans loved Shirley, but some others could be mean and jealous. Unkind rumors spread as soon as Shirley began work on her second major movie, *Little Miss Marker,* in 1934. Because she was such a good actress, some people suggested that she was actually an adult who only *looked* like a child because she was a midget. They said Gertrude was a pushy mother who forced her daughter to work hard so *she* could get money and status from Shirley's success.

Actually, Shirley was the one who looked forward to working each day. She would complain and worry when her mother got dressed too slowly or took too long with her make-up.

Shirley didn't think her daily schedule of rehearsals, filming, music lessons, and magazine interviews was at all unusual. It was the only way of life she knew. Looking back on it today, she still says she enjoyed every minute of it.

Six days a week, she and her mother were driven to the movie studio by her bodyguard, Grif. His job was to protect Shirley from possible kidnappers and to make sure that she was brought safely to the studio by nine o'clock every morning—even when she was not making a film.

On the studio grounds, the company president had built a pretty little four-room cottage especially for Shirley. It was surrounded by a real picket fence. The yard had a tree swing, a garden, and a pen for Shirley's pet rabbits.

The cottage had its own kitchen so Shirley wouldn't have to eat lunch in the regular cafeteria.

Studio executives worried that adults would change her innocent nature or give her so many sweets she would become too chubby.

In her cottage bedroom, Shirley took regular afternoon naps, just like any other little girl. All of the furniture, including a piano, was painted white, and built to her size.

Another room in the cottage was a combination office and schoolroom. By California law, the studio had to be sure Shirley spent at least three hours each weekday on her studies.

Her favorite tutor, a young woman known as "Klammie," realized right away that Shirley's lessons would have to be special. Using maps and books, she took the story of whatever film Shirley was working on and related it to the real world of history and geography. When Shirley entered politics as an adult, she recalled how Klammie's clever teaching method had focused her interest on the problems of people all around the world. But even Klammie couldn't manage to make math seem interesting. That was one subject Shirley never liked!

Young Shirley's career as an actress blossomed quickly. By the mid-1930s, she had become very used to daily routine at the studio, and very comfortable in her little cottage.

The Shirley Temple movies began to appear regularly, each better than the last. Audiences of all ages loved seeing Shirley on the big screen. And Shirley loved being a movie star. But behind the glamour was a difficult schedule: filming in the morning, lunch, a thirty-minute nap, schoolwork, more filming in the late afternoon, and then more schoolwork to end the day.

Shirley's only playmates were the adult members of the film crew, who all liked her very much. Although she looked like an angel with her charming smiles and frilly dresses, Shirley was a normal child who liked to fool around and play jokes. Sometimes Gertrude had to use her sternest voice and say, "Be good, Shirley!" Then her daughter would instantly behave.

Shirley had a wonderful time during the filming of *Little Miss Marker*. For this movie, she was *supposed to* misbehave! And she had to act in all kinds of "dangerous" scenes. Actually, these scenes just *looked* dangerous. They were really very safe—and lots of fun. At one point in the filming, everyone watched nervously as Shirley was "thrown" from a horse. But she didn't actually fall—instead, she was whisked up to the ceiling, out of the camera's view, by an invisible harness.

Gertrude and the studio executives may have been nervous about Shirley's safety, but Shirley couldn't have been happier! The horse, a very gentle animal called Dream Prince, had been taught to back up on two legs so his tiny rider would fly into the air, jerked upward by the harness wires. "You're supposed to be scared," the director complained when Shirley couldn't seem to stop smiling.

Shirley enjoyed acting so much that some adult actors complained she liked it *too* much. As her co-star in *Little Miss Marker* put it, "She knows all the tricks. She . . . grabs my laughs. She's making a stooge out of me!"

Shirley didn't know what he was talking about. She didn't realize that the jealous actor thought she was purposely "stealing" the scenes, or taking attention away from him. As far as Shirley was concerned, she was just doing what she'd been trained to do: the best job possible.

Many people still didn't really take Shirley's acting skill seriously because she was a child. On this very picture, the director just assumed Shirley wouldn't be able to act out a sad scene, so he played a terrible trick on her. In the story, Shirley's character, Miss Marker, was supposed to cry. To be sure Shirley had *real* tears in her eyes, the director told Gertrude to leave the movie set. Then he secretly ordered the cameras to start rolling. "Shirley," he announced, "your mother has been kidnapped by an ugly man, all green with blood-red eyes." Shirley began crying so hard she couldn't stop. When Gertrude returned, she was furious with the director for upsetting her daughter so needlessly.

Shirley didn't have to be tricked into crying! Gertrude and Shirley had developed their own technique for acting out sad scenes. Before going to sleep, Shirley would listen carefully as Gertrude read aloud the next day's "crying scene." The next morning, Shirley would wake up in a serious mood, and no one at home or at the studio would interrupt her thoughts. When the scene began, she would blank out all thoughts and concentrate on crying.

This way of practicing worked perfectly for Shirley. Other actors often had to put drops in their eyes that looked like tears, but Shirley could always produce the real thing!

One problem with Shirley's method, of course, was that all her crying scenes had to be scheduled in the morning. By afternoon, her natural good spirits would take over, and it would be almost impossible to get her back in a serious mood.

By the time of her next film, *Baby Take a Bow*, six-year-old Shirley was as popular as the Fox movie company's best-loved adult stars.

That same year, Shirley made a movie called *Now and Forever*. She starred with one of America's most famous actors, who quickly became her good friend. Gary Cooper gave Shirley the nickname "Wiggle-Britches" and brought her lovely toys, including a wind-up walking white cat. The actor was also a talented artist, and he taught Shirley how to draw.

But it was her next film, *Bright Eyes*, which brought Shirley her greatest success so far. In this movie she danced down the aisle of an airplane, and sang, "On the Good Ship Lollipop!" The song was an instant hit. People everywhere bought the music so they could play and sing it by themselves at home.

During the filming of *Bright Eyes*, someone started a silly rumor that Shirley's curls were not real—that they had been attached by a wigmaker! In fact, Gertrude pinned up her daughter's hair every night, making exactly fifty-six curls. If she didn't do this, Shirley's hair would become frizzy in the wet ocean air of Santa Monica.

Shirley and Gertrude had more important things to think about than idle gossip, however. At about this time, plans were being made to bring Shirley together with her best loved, and most unlikely, co-star. This talented little girl was still only six years old, but she was about to become a world-famous figure.

Darlin' and Uncle Billy

By 1934, Shirley's films were so popular that the Fox movie studio could hardly keep up with the demand for new ones. Because she was known as "one-take" Shirley—meaning she rarely made a mistake that required shooting a scene more than once—a Shirley Temple movie could be completed in only six or seven weeks.

Shirley was now making so much money that her parents were able to buy a larger house and hire housekeeping help. Neighborhood friends were invited to the new house to play every Sunday, Shirley's only day off, but she was never allowed to visit them. The Great Depression was getting even worse. And as Shirley's fame and fortune grew, so did her mother's fears that her daughter would be kidnapped and held for ransom.

On vacation trips to sunny Palm Springs, Shirley spent as much time being photographed by reporters and adoring fans as she did actually having fun. But as far as Shirley was concerned, stardom *was* fun!

Meanwhile, back in Hollywood, the moviemakers were hard at work, looking for ways to make Shirley an even bigger star. One of them came up with a daring idea.

At this period in American history, black people were not accepted as equals by most parts of white society. In much of the country, including the armed services, the rules of segregation kept white and black people separate from one another.

Some black performers did get jobs in films, but they played minor roles of servants, musicians, dancers, and comedians. A black actor hardly ever starred in a film made for white audiences. And no one had ever paired a young white actress with a black adult actor. But this is exactly what happened when Shirley Temple and Bill Robinson were hired to make *The Little Colonel*. When this match was announced, no one knew if it would be successful or not. Some people thought audiences would be captivated by the unlikely duo. Others feared they'd be outraged.

In fact, Shirley and Bill "Bojangles" Robinson danced straight into America's heart. Graceful and powerful, the handsome Robinson lit up the movie screen. A true professional, he had many new dance steps and techniques to teach his young partner.

During the filming, Shirley grew to love her "Uncle Billy," as she called him. Robinson was amazed by the little girl's abilities. He called Shirley "Darlin'" and practiced the dance steps over and over with her until she could almost do them in her sleep. Once, he gently kissed Shirley's feet and said, "Uncle Billy doesn't tell her feet where to go, her heart tells her."

One of the most famous dance routines in movie history is their remarkable "staircase dance" in *The Little Colonel*. Shirley and Bill tapped, kicked, scuffled, and did a triple-time race up and down a set of steps to produce an unforgettable performance.

During filming, Shirley spent as much time as possible with her co-star, who was a wonderful storyteller. He introduced her to a whole new world, telling her all about the hidden light of diamonds in African mines.

Shirley's parents had never told her about racial prejudice, and they welcomed Bill Robinson and his wife into their home. In the entertainment world, performers of both races often mixed easily, despite the feelings of some of their fans.

Even though the film became a smashing success, several scenes that showed the black actor and white actress touching had to be cut, or taken out of the movie. Many fans who saw the first showings of the film before it officially opened, objected to the closeness between the actors. The audience even disapproved when Shirley and Bill lightly touched fingers in the dance on the stairs.

Shirley didn't know that Bill Robinson, who was then considered the best dancer in the country, was not allowed to use the same doors, elevators, or restrooms as his white co-stars and fans. She didn't understand why some people thought she and "Uncle Billy" shouldn't be friends. But she did have a direct experience with racial prejudice that quickly opened her eyes.

Rehearsals for *The Little Colonel* were held in Palm Springs, where Shirley and her parents stayed in an elegant hotel. Each family had a separate cottage—not just a separate room—and Shirley was puzzled when she couldn't find Bill Robinson's cottage. She was very upset when she learned the reason why: he was staying in a room above a nearby drugstore. This was where the hotel workers, personal maids, and the chauffeurs (including his own) had to sleep. Even though he was a famous, wealthy man, "Uncle Billy" was not allowed to stay in the same cottages as the white families.

Shirley was still a child, but she was beginning to learn that the fantasy world of the movie studio was nothing like real life.

By 1935, Shirley's life with the studio seemed like a fantasy indeed. Judging by the number of tickets sold, she was the top film star in the entire world! The profits from her movies had saved Fox from bankruptcy. Even though people had very little money to spend because of the Great Depression, they still bought tickets to see Shirley's films. To show its appreciation, the Motion Picture Academy of Arts and Sciences gave her a special "Oscar." It was a real honor, but Shirley was disappointed because her Oscar was made smaller than those given to adult actors. She never liked being treated as a child, especially in her work, so the child-size statuette was just about meaningless to her.

But, Shirley had no complaints about her daily work. During this year, she made *Our Little Girl.*

Right after that, she made *Curly Top,* playing herself at several stages of life in a song called "When I Grow Up." Then she gladly rejoined Bill Robinson for *The Littlest Rebel,* a serious story in which her character pleads with President Lincoln to save her father's life. The best part of making this movie was that the script writer knew Shirley was an expert with a slingshot, and he added a scene in the film just so she could show off her skill!

Meanwhile, the Temple family moved again, now that Shirley was making so much money. In their big, new house, they began a life-style that would lead to problems in the future.

Life at the Top

During the time Shirley grew up, the Los Angeles area was surrounded by trees and undeveloped farmland. In a beautiful hilly area above their Santa Monica house, Shirley's parents bought four acres with a fine view of the sparkling Pacific Ocean and the Catalina Channel.

The Temples had a luxurious estate built there—a large country house with a swimming pool, horse stables, and a modest guest cottage nearby. There was even a child-sized roller coaster and merry-go-round! All of this was surrounded by a chain-link fence and a stone wall. Guards were on duty twenty-four hours a day. The windows and doors were electrically wired to the nearest police station, in case a burglar tried to enter the house. The Temples had so much money now, they were more afraid than ever that somebody might rob their house or kidnap Shirley.

Eventually, it took as many as twelve servants and a whole lot of money to run this impressive household. Shirley herself received an allowance of four dollars each week.

At this time, when George Temple did not get a promotion he felt he deserved, he quit his job at the bank to become the manager of Shirley's earnings. Gertrude thought this was a fine idea. Like her daughter, who didn't care much for mathematics, Mrs. Temple did not trust herself with numbers. She believed her husband was an expert. Shirley, of course, didn't question her parents' decision.

Shirley loved her father, she explained when she was older, but she always understood his good points *and* his bad points. George was lovable and fatherly, but he could be easily fooled by fast-talking, powerful businessmen. Even when she was a child, Shirley understood that he always needed to feel important. And this sometimes got him into trouble.

In the 1930s, the Temples were one of the few families in the whole country who did not have to worry about money. Gertrude spent as much as she liked on clothes, and George always gave money to friends who needed it. Shirley's parents gave her whatever she asked for, and fans from all over the world often sent her expensive presents.

It seemed that this way of life would never end. The president of the Fox studio, Darryl Zanuck, called Shirley "the greatest star in our business" and predicted that she would "go on forever." Her salary was higher than his, and more than the salaries of many famous adult movie stars! In 1936, according to one estimate, Shirley made *fifteen times* her regular salary from products that used her name, such as dolls, cups, and lunch boxes.

Shirley's reputation grew and grew.

Eager fans couldn't wait to see her next movie, *Captain January*. Audiences especially loved watching her dance among baskets of lobsters. They might have enjoyed her Hawaiian hula dance as well, but it was cut from the film because some people thought it was too "indecent" for America's favorite little girl.

In *Poor Little Rich Girl,* Shirley played a wealthy child without any close friends. Many people thought the movie was probably based on her real life. The story had a happy ending, of course, and is considered one of Shirley's best films. With two other actors, she danced a complicated tap routine to the song "I Love a Military Man." That number is often used as an example of movie dancing at its best.

In *Dimples*, named for Shirley's very own dimples, she came up against a difficult co-star in Frank Morgan, the actor who later played the wizard in *The Wizard of Oz*. He liked to steal a scene as much as Shirley did, and the two were soon competing with one another.

When Shirley was talking, Frank Morgan would sometimes move around in a way that was meant to distract audiences from watching his co-star. Frustrated by this, Shirley soon began to fight back, creating minor distractions of her own. One actress became so interested in watching the two vie for attention that she forgot a whole speech! For one of Shirley's songs, the annoyed film director made Mr. Morgan turn his back to the camera so the audience couldn't see him at all! *Dimples* is not an especially well-known film, but it is entertaining to watch the two stars working so hard to steal each other's scenes!

After Shirley's next movie, *Stowaway*, the studio executives began to worry. Their child star was growing up. She was now nine years old—though she and everyone else except her family thought she was only eight. She would not be able to play an adorable little girl much longer.

But that was okay with Shirley. She was eager to play the part of an older girl, too. She wanted to try something new.

At the same time, Gertrude was becoming bored with the daily routine at the studio. Shirley might still enjoy herself, but her mother had a difficult job to do. She had to make sure Shirley was prepared in every way, and to keep constant watch during the long days of filming and rehearsal. Sometimes, when Shirley couldn't understand what the movie director wanted, Gertrude had to explain his orders. That meant she had to pay close attention at all times during the filming. And Shirley relied on her for so many things—especially to set the proper mood for each scene.

In addition, many famous people wanted to meet Shirley, and Gertrude had to plan their visits around her daughter's busy schedule. Nearly every day, Shirley received hundreds of requests for autographs. Almost as many people called or wrote to see if Shirley would make a special appearance on behalf of one charity or another. Sometimes all of these demands grew tiresome—especially for Gertrude.

Shirley now had thousands of adoring fans. When she appeared in public, the crowds often pushed and shoved, eager to catch a glimpse of their tiny idol or to touch her. Sometimes their enthusiasm was frightening. Shirley's fans could become quite rude and angry if Shirley and Gertrude tried to hurry by.

Gertrude Temple had always kept a careful watch on Shirley's public "image." She approved every script before allowing Shirley to accept a role. But as she began to tire of all the responsibilities and as Shirley grew older, Gertrude stopped being so careful. She looked toward the Fox studio, and Mr. Zanuck, for help in shaping Shirley's changing career.

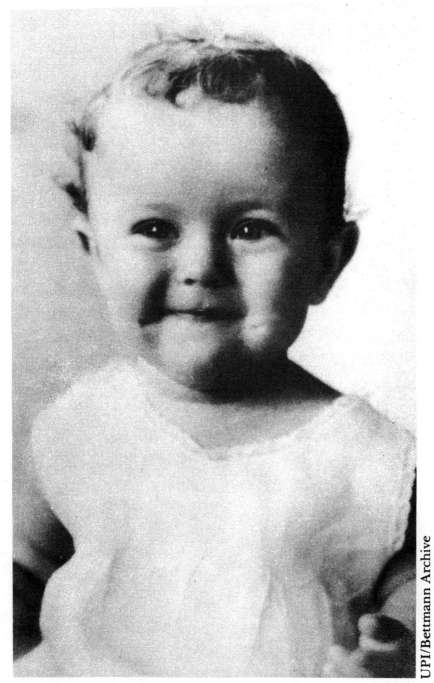

Baby Shirley

Culver Pictures

Shirley and Bill "Bojangles" Robinson in a scene from
The Little Colonel (1934).

AP/Wide World Photos

Shirley practices her lines with her mother before facing
the camera.

Shirley meets Eleanor Roosevelt, the wife of President Franklin D. Roosevelt.

Shirley and her costars on the set of the 1934 movie,
Stand Up and Cheer.

Shirley in a scene from *Heidi* **(1937).**

Shirley and Bill Robinson delight their audiences with a dance in *Just Around the Corner* **(1939).**

Shirley attempts to free her costar in *Baby Take a Bow* (1934).

Shirley and her parents, George and Gertrude, in 1948.

Shirley shares a soda with her first husband, John Agar.

Shirley gets serious on the set of *Wee Willie Winkie* (1937).

A movie theater proudly presents Shirley's 1935 film, *Curly Top.*

Shirley poses with the "old" Shirley Temple doll (right) and the new version (left) in 1957.

**Shirley Temple Black and her husband, Charles Black,
on vacation in Bermuda.**

Shirley at work at the United Nations.

Sygma

Shirley signing copies of her autobiography at a bookstore in New York City.

Triumphs and Rocky Days

"**F**or two years Shirley has been doing the same thing," complained one movie critic. "Give her more intelligent stories, Mr. Zanuck, and better actors in supporting roles."

Darryl Zanuck, the Fox studio boss, didn't need the critics to tell him that Shirley was ready for something new. And he already had something special in mind.

The two pictures Shirley made in 1937 were instant winners. Mr. Zanuck cast her with adult movie stars noted for fine acting. He also hired some of the industry's best directors. Shirley would have to "stretch," as actors call it. That meant she would have to show greater emotional depth than ever before. And everyone who knew Shirley thought she'd have no problem handling her new roles.

In *Wee Willie Winkie*, Shirley was still a bubbly, curly-headed young girl, but she had to show a slightly more serious side. The movie script was based on a well-known tale by Rudyard Kipling. The hero of the book was a boy who lived in British-ruled India. In the movie, however, the main character was changed to a girl—and played by Shirley!

There were some very rough moments in the filming of *Wee Willie Winkie*, but Shirley enjoyed them all. The cast included an aging elephant and a bad-tempered camel. For almost a month, Shirley was filmed in the desert, forty miles from Los Angeles. Shirley got right into the rough-and-ready spirit of the tale. In one scene, in fact, she punched one of the actors so hard that they had to refilm the scene and warn her to be a little bit more gentle!

When a horse on the set reared on cue and dropped its rider at Shirley's feet, she didn't even flinch. She was equally calm when a lantern near her shattered from a rifle bullet. And when an actress was afraid to spank her, as the script required, Shirley insisted on *really* being spanked!

Well aware of his feisty young star's courage by now, the director decided to try Shirley in a dangerous scene. Normally, for a scene like this, an actor's "double" would be used. A double is someone who is dressed up to look like the real actor, but is actually trained to perform difficult stunts.

For this scene, Shirley had to run across a path of stampeding horses and climb up a pile of rocks to safety. If she tripped and fell, or slipped while climbing, the horses could trample her. Although Gertrude was quite worried, Shirley couldn't wait to meet this challenge. When the cameras started rolling, she raced in front of the thundering herd and scrambled up the rocks with no problem at all! She was very proud of herself. In her mind she had convinced everybody that she was as professional and brave as any adult actor. And as far as the public was concerned, Shirley's acting had taken a giant step forward!

Shirley's next film, *Heidi*, was based on another popular book. Shirley and the cast traveled to the wooded slopes of Lake Arrowhead in California to film the scenes that were supposedly set in the Swiss Alps. Working outside was a welcome change from the studio.

At the studio, they had filmed a snowy street scene under a huge tent using fake snow. To moviegoers, it would look like an actual winter night. But in reality, the set was so hot that the actor who played Heidi's grandfather fainted.

Even though Shirley became ill from the artificial snow, she still had a wonderful time filming *Heidi*. She loved holding the reins as she sped through a narrow archway on a carriage horse. She thought it was great fun to be butted from behind by a goat called Old Turk. And she was annoyed when Gertrude called a halt after several takes and forced the director to use a double—a boy, no less—for some other difficult scenes.

When Shirley couldn't milk a nanny goat successfully, a long thin tube (hidden from the camera) was attached to the goat so milk would squirt out automatically. But no one told Shirley about this. When no milk came, she put her face up to the goat's belly and examined it closely to see if there was a problem. Then all of a sudden, out came the milk, squirting a surprised Shirley in the face! Although it wasn't in the script, the scene was so naturally funny that the director kept it in the film.

Shirley's fans loved her new movies. Before *Heidi* was even completed, she was named the top box-office star for the third year in a row. Young Shirley, just nine years old, was chosen by American women as their favorite actress.

This surprised some people, but it revealed the secret of Shirley's success. Young as she was, she never appeared in movies that were made only for children. Her films were written, cast, and directed to appeal to viewers of all ages.

But even at the height of her fame, Shirley and her mother could see trouble looming ahead. A new young film star, Sonja Henie, world ice-skating champion from Norway, was about to overshadow Shirley. Sonja's acting was not very good, but her skating was magical. She dazzled audiences with her flying leaps and graceful spins. In 1938, her films made twice as much money as Shirley's for the Fox studio. As the profits poured in from Sonja's films, Mr. Zanuck became less interested in finding just the right scripts for Shirley.

Her next three films, *Rebecca of Sunnybrook Farm*, *Little Miss Broadway*, and *Just Around the Corner*, were lively and entertaining, but they were too similar to her earlier films. Shirley needed more fresh, new material.

Finally, Mr. Zanuck found a good script, *The Little Princess*, for Shirley's first full-color film. The story was set in 1899, and the movie crew was careful to capture every detail of the time period—especially the costumes. Shirley had to wear seven layers of skirts and petticoats, just like girls of that era. Her cotton undergarments were decorated with bows, lace, and ruffles! And her hair was arranged in an older, more mature style.

As always, Shirley was eager to begin. But once on the set, she began to notice a change in the way people treated her. The other actors were jealous of her, and they made no effort to hide their feelings. Under their critical gaze, Shirley became suddenly self-conscious. She was embarrassed when she didn't perform properly in a ballet sequence. And somehow, she even felt responsible when a monkey bit her during rehearsals.

Now that Shirley was a teenager, many things in her personal life and in her acting career were changing. But she had no idea how drastic those changes would turn out to be.

Early "Retirement"

Both fans and critics raved about *The Little Princess*. Shirley was so good that another studio offered to pay her *twice* her usual salary to play the role of Dorothy in *The Wizard of Oz*. But Mr. Zanuck didn't want Shirley to leave Fox. He starred her, instead, in a dull, black and white frontier adventure called *Susannah of the Mounties*. Unlike Shirley's other movies, it appealed only to small children.

Shirley enjoyed working on the film with the Blackfoot Indian chiefs. She was thrilled when the twelve native Americans, led by Chief Mad Plume, voted to make her a "blood-sister." And she was too excited to feel any pain when Chief Yellow Kidney pricked their fingers with a penknife and pressed the bloody cuts together. But even though Shirley had fun and made some good friends during the filming, the movie was not a great success. "Shirley's growing up, but her stories aren't," one newspaper reported when *Susannah* premiered.

Meanwhile, Judy Garland had landed the lead in *The Wizard of Oz* and enchanted audiences everywhere. She became the fifth most popular movie star in the United States, while Shirley sank to number thirteen. Things got so bad that the Shirley Temple dolls were discontinued since hardly anyone was buying them anymore. Mr. Zanuck didn't know what to do. He offered a prize of $25,000 to anyone who could come up with a good story for Shirley's next film.

Gertrude couldn't help worrying about Shirley's career, though she did nothing to control the family's spending during this time. George Temple was having trouble with Shirley's financial affairs. He was involved in many lawsuits with people who claimed they deserved part of Shirley's earnings.

On the brighter side, the Temple family took advantage of the lull in Shirley's work schedule to visit Hawaii, her favorite vacation spot. There she frolicked in the ocean and joined the local kids in softball games. It was a rare and much needed break for the hard-working young actress.

Finally, late in 1939, Mr. Zanuck decided that *The Blue Bird* would be the answer to Shirley's problems. *The Blue Bird* was an imaginative story filled with fantastic characters, based on a well-known theatrical masterpiece. But for some reason, the story didn't come across as well on film as it had in the theater.

Part of the problem was that Shirley had to play a selfish and cruel character. No matter how skillfully she acted, she couldn't please her fans in this role. In addition, rumors of war were sweeping across Europe. People had no time for fairy tales now—real world issues were too troubling.

Whatever the reason, *The Blue Bird* was a failure. And Shirley's next film, *Young People,* was an even worse disaster. This story used scenes from Shirley's old films and ended with her character's retirement from show business before she became a teenager. One of the songs from the movie is "Auld Lang Syne," the well-known Scottish song of farewell. Some people thought this was a hint that Fox was planning to let Shirley go. Gertrude angrily denied rumors that Shirley, like her character in the movie, also wanted to retire. And Mr. and Mrs. Temple fought with studio executives about Shirley's contract. Eventually, however, the business relationship came to an end. Shirley's career with the Fox studio was over.

By age eleven, Shirley had worked at Fox for two-thirds of her life. Her twenty-two pictures earned over thirty million dollars in profits for the company. When she and her mother went to clean out her studio cottage, a teary-eyed cleaning woman looked on. "Is this the way they do with a star?" she asked. "I've just outgrown it, that's all," Shirley replied, smiling sadly.

Although Gertrude was upset that studios did not immediately try to hire her daughter, Shirley looked forward to finally leading the kind of life she had never had—a "normal" one.

For the first time, now, she attended a school with other children. At the Westlake School for Girls, she was just another student, with no special privileges. She had to learn how to make new friends. Many of her classmates had known each other for years and had formed tight groups. Some came from very wealthy, snobbish families and looked down on show business people. No one seemed at all impressed that Shirley was a movie star. The other girls were more interested in grades and social position.

All of this was just fine with Shirley. She wanted to be accepted for her personal qualities rather than her professional achievements. She felt sure she could overcome the snobbery of the other girls.

After a slow start, Shirley did develop her own group of friends. They loved to visit the Temple estate for swimming parties and horseback riding. The girls were thrilled to dress up for Shirley's twelfth birthday party at a country club in the fashionable town of Bel-Air. Like Shirley, her friends were amazed to discover that it was actually her *thirteenth* birthday! The unexpected extra year was the best birthday present Shirley could have—she was a teenager, at last!

To Shirley, growing up meant a new interest: boys. She had always played happily with her older brothers and the boys on the movie set. Now she and her new friends became fascinated with make-up and nice clothes. Before long, Shirley had many boyfriends. She was so pleased by the attention that she refused to choose just one!

To her parents, however, Shirley's social life was of little importance. It was her career that concerned them. Soon, they signed a contract with

Metro-Goldwyn-Mayer (MGM), a big movie company willing to update Shirley's "image."

MGM promised to find scripts for a young woman—not a little girl. Unfortunately, the movie they chose for Shirley, *Kathleen,* was not a very good one. And when it didn't do well at the box office, the studio quickly dropped her.

Another producer then signed her for *Miss Annie Rooney,* but for once Shirley wasn't eager to begin a new film. She didn't like interrupting her life at school, and the movie did nothing for her career. In fact, it is remembered only because Shirley received her first on-screen kiss in it. This was a big change in her image, though the famous kiss was just a gentle peck on the cheek. The film itself was so silly that Shirley didn't receive another offer for almost a year and a half.

Meanwhile, Shirley happily continued her education in schoolwork and teen romance. But the coming world war would soon affect her carefree life. One of her brothers had joined the Marines and been sent to the South Pacific to fight. Her other brother was in the Army Air Corps. Some of her boyfriends entered military training, too.

As the war went on, Shirley received letters from lonely servicemen of all ages. She seemed to remind them of their sisters, daughters, and girl-friends back home. She hired two secretaries to help answer the letters, and she began visiting wounded soldiers at hospitals regularly. She often attended rallies for the war effort as well.

Suddenly, Shirley was offered a role in a movie about the problems faced by families left behind when men went off to war. In *Since You Went Away*, she acted with many fine movie stars. Scrubbed clean of make-up and with her hair bobbed, Shirley was called "charming" by critics. This was her first serious young adult part, and she was a great success.

Performing with more experienced actors taught Shirley many new lessons, some of which were not so easy. No longer the center of attention, she had to learn to be part of the group and to cope with unkind remarks and jealousy from her co-stars. Shirley was a big girl now and couldn't always rely on her mother for protection. This was a real change for Shirley.

But the most important change was a happy one: a seven-year contract! Shirley was named the year's "most promising newcomer," and her comeback seemed complete.

As soon as her contract was signed, she made *I'll*

Be Seeing You. The picture was not a huge hit, but Shirley was again praised for her fine acting and her new, mature screen personality. In *Kiss and Tell,* the finest film of her "second career," she was called "quite extraordinary." And yet Shirley's professional and personal lives were about to change overnight—again.

Marriage

Competitive in all things, Shirley decided to be the first person in her Westlake class to become engaged. She hadn't yet chosen the lucky man, but she was sure she'd have no problem finding a suitable candidate.

As it turned out, Shirley fell in love at the poolside in her own backyard. John Agar was the tall, dark, handsome older brother of a classmate. At 6'2", he was precisely the height of her two brothers, a coincidence that appealed to Shirley. A slim, blue-eyed athlete with a square jaw, John looked extremely handsome in his Army Air Corps uniform. But he had one special characteristic that really pleased Shirley: He seemed to know little, and care less, about films.

At the time, the fighting in World War II was bloody. John Agar would soon be sent overseas, perhaps never to return. Shirley was sixteen years old and about to graduate from high school. She had no plans to attend college, and there were no new film opportunities on the horizon. John and Shirley decided to get married.

A war-weary world joyfully received the news that Shirley Temple, America's princess, was going to marry an all-American soldier. The wedding took place on September 19, 1945, and drew a crowd of 12,000 to the streets outside the church! Radiant in white satin and pearls, Shirley was the picture of happiness as she walked down the aisle. A twelve-foot satin train trailed behind her.

As the church doors flew open after the ceremony, the eager crowd outside pushed forward to get closer to Shirley. Police had to form a circle of protection around the newlyweds, and some bridesmaids had pieces of their dresses torn off for souvenirs.

Sadly, there was more unpleasantness that night. By mistake, police reported that the Agars had been killed in a car accident. The frantic Temple family didn't learn the truth for twenty-four hours. To make things worse, the hotel lost the reservations for the couple's wedding night. When a room was finally found, the Agars began their first night as husband and wife with a terrible quarrel.

Shirley was very independent, but she had never really been on her own. After the honeymoon, she moved with her husband into the guest cottage beside her parents' pool. Gertrude and George, only a few yards away, could see and hear much of what went on between the Agars. John probably felt uncomfortable being so close to his in-laws, but Shirley was happy with the arrangement.

After his discharge from the service, John didn't seem at all eager to find a job. Gossip columnists began calling him "Mr. Shirley Temple," meaning that he was supported by his wife's movie work.

The young couple might have been better off on their own. But Shirley liked comfort, household help, clothes, and spending money. And John liked expensive restaurants and late-night dance clubs.

Though she was now a grown woman, Shirley still depended on a small allowance from her father. He never explained to her how much money she had or how much she could spend. Shirley assumed that all the money she had earned over the years had been put safely aside for her personal use when she reached the age of twenty-one. She had no idea that hardly any of that money was left.

Meanwhile, Shirley was working on a film called *Honeymoon*. She earned a good salary, but the reviews were bad.

Shirley's personal life seemed to be affecting her ability to act. The Agar marriage was troubled by one argument after another. John often drank heavily and would become either quiet or moody. Shirley often left the dinner table in tears. Once, a cook who was angry with John for treating Shirley poorly, attacked him with a butcher knife.

When the couple went to parties or nightclubs, John would leave Shirley by herself and dance or flirt with other women. Hoping to keep him home, Shirley welcomed John's friends at the cottage, but they either ignored her or rudely demanded food and drinks. Sometimes, John would stay out all night. When he returned, he wouldn't tell Shirley where he had been.

Then he made an announcement that surprised and worried Shirley. Though he had no experience, he suddenly decided to become an actor. Shirley knew that two-actor marriages often didn't last. Still, she wished him well and kept her doubts to herself.

While her husband began his career in film, Shirley co-starred with future President of the United States Ronald Reagan in *That Hagen Girl.* Critics called the movie "uninspired soap opera," and described Shirley's acting as "wooden." To some people, this film marked the beginning of the end of Shirley's career as an adult actress.

Next, Shirley and her husband both appeared in a movie called *Fort Apache.* The film starred John Wayne, Henry Fonda, and other fine actors. It made a lot of money, but the Agars, who played a young couple in love, were barely noticed.

Just as her movie career seemed to be ending, Shirley's personal life offered her a new beginning. She was going to have a baby! Soon she would once again delight her loyal fans with another new achievement: the birth of a beautiful daughter, Susan. What her adoring public didn't know was that Shirley had driven herself to the hospital in the early morning hours, carrying her own suitcase. After taking sleeping pills, John was in too deep a sleep to help.

Still, the baby seemed to strengthen the Agars' failing marriage. Shirley loved motherhood, and she was in no hurry to return to work. But when she and John were both offered parts in *Adventure in Baltimore,* she accepted the role for his sake. The job was fun, but the movie was not very good.

Shirley made three movies without John in 1949, but none of them did well. In fact, each one made her former popularity seem more like a distant memory. At the Fox studio, she made *Mr. Belvedere Goes to College.* This movie was not successful either. And memories of the stardom she had once enjoyed at Fox were painful.

Meanwhile, John made a movie called *She Wore a Yellow Ribbon,* which was very popular. The film did well at the box office, and many people began to think he might have a long career ahead of him. He began to enjoy the privileges of stardom, including party invitations and the attention of admiring women.

At about this time, Shirley made a tough decision. For months, she had been considering a divorce. Then, one night, she took baby Susan and left the cottage. When John arrived home, he found Shirley's lawyer waiting with the news. Shirley refused to talk with John about it at all, or to see him ever again.

Shirley won her divorce and custody of Susan but lost a lot of her fans in the process. She received no more movie offers, and her Hollywood friends suddenly disappeared. Shirley was lonely and sad, living with her daughter in the little cottage by the pool. Many people now said she was truly "washed up."

For a much-needed vacation, Shirley decided to take Susan and her parents to Hawaii. The sea breezes, rich greenery, and quiet beaches would help her forget her troubles. And she had old friends there who didn't care that she was no longer a star.

It was through her friends in Hawaii that Shirley met Charles Black, the man who is still her husband today. A natural athlete and a decorated war hero, Charles was the son of a wealthy San Francisco businessman. He was nine years older than Shirley and had never seen any of her movies. Shirley was relieved that Charles didn't like her for her fame, but she had to admit she wished he'd seen at least *one* Shirley Temple film!

The romance blossomed, and Shirley stayed in Hawaii much longer than she had planned. Reporters were curious, but she and Charles were able to keep their love a secret. Unsuccessful in her first marriage, Shirley needed time to consider this unexpected change in her life. She hadn't gone to

Hawaii to fall in love, but that's exactly what happened.

Shirley and Charles finally decided that this was indeed the real thing. After escaping publicity for almost a year, they invited a small group of family and friends to celebrate their wedding on December 16, 1950.

Shirley then told reporters that her nineteen years of moviemaking were definitely over. "My only contract is with Mr. Black . . . and it's exclusive!"

New Challenges

Although Shirley's life had always been touched with fantasy and make-believe, the real world of politics could not be ignored as she grew older.

There was now a war being fought in North Korea, and Charles had to return to the Navy. When he was stationed in Washington, D.C., Shirley set up housekeeping in a tiny apartment there. The Blacks' life wasn't glamorous, but it was always fun and interesting. Important friends of Charles's parents often invited the young couple to dinner parties, where Shirley met many people who worked for the government. Some of them were in a position to make decisions that would change the course of history. Shirley saw how fulfilling it might be to become active in politics.

During this time, Shirley was recovering from a shocking discovery—a secret that the public wouldn't learn until she published her autobiography in 1988. Shirley had always believed that millions of dollars from her movie career had been set aside for her future. She assumed that she would never have to worry about money because she had earned so much from her films. By law, her father was required to put at least $800,000 aside for her. The rest of Shirley's money was supposedly safely invested.

In fact, Shirley's father had badly mismanaged her affairs. Millions of dollars had simply vanished. He seemed unable to explain the disappearance of the money, and Shirley didn't press him for an answer. It was clear to her that the money was gone for good, and she didn't want it to destroy her relationship with her father.

All Shirley actually had was $40,000 and the guest cottage. She sold the cottage and used the money to buy a house in rural Maryland near the nation's capital.

The public was amazed that she "chose" to live so modestly. They didn't know that she could no longer afford her former life-style, including the tight security that had protected her in California. At least once in her adult life, she had to rely on her own quick thinking to foil a kidnapping attempt. Once, a strange man tried to force his way into the house. Shirley used her acting ability to convince him that Charles was home, and then she alerted the police. It turned out that the man and an accomplice were planning to take baby Susan for ransom.

But a worse threat to Shirley's life came from the birth of her second child in 1952. After delivering Charles Jr., she became very ill. It took Shirley seven long weeks to regain enough strength to return home with her newborn son.

About then, Shirley's father became seriously ill, too. And one of her brothers learned he had multiple sclerosis, an incurable disease of the nervous system.

But Shirley had new concerns and ambitions to keep her mind off her personal problems. When General Dwight David Eisenhower ran as the Republican candidate for President, the Blacks worked hard on his campaign. At the same time, they became friends with Eisenhower's running-mate, Richard M. Nixon.

After the election, the Blacks returned to California for a few years of quiet family life. Their daughter, Lori, was born there in 1954. Preferring calm, suburban northern California to hectic Hollywood, Shirley and Charles decided to make their home in Atherton. The town wasn't far from Charles's new job as the director of business administration at the Stanford Research Institute.

Once again, Shirley began receiving film offers, and now television producers were interested in her, too. Television was still growing in popularity at this time, and the networks couldn't develop new shows fast enough to satisfy the public demand. Shirley kept saying no until NBC created a series that she liked. Even then, she set limits on the amount of time she would spend at the Los Angeles studio. She actually held a family vote before accepting the offer: Charles and the three children were unanimously in favor of her becoming a TV star!

The television show, *Shirley Temple's Storybook,* ran successfully from January through December of 1958. Shirley acted in only three of the episodes. More often, she appeared as narrator, or storyteller, for the plays the show featured. The series was so popular that she was able to make a deal with a toy company to produce a new Shirley Temple doll. And once again, such products as Shirley Temple clothing and books were sold in stores across the country.

Despite her success with a new generation of fans, Shirley never did very much television acting. Instead, she found herself following a very different calling—one that had appealed to her years earlier when she was living in Washington.

Actors with whom she had once worked, like Ronald Reagan and George Murphy, were becoming successful in politics. Shirley began to speak so often on behalf of the Republican Party and various charities that many people wondered why she didn't run for public office herself.

By 1967, Shirley's children were all teenagers. She was now very active in northern California political affairs, and had been appointed to the state's Advisory Hospital Council by Governor Ronald Reagan. So when her Congressman died unexpectedly in 1967, leaving an unfinished term of office to be filled, Shirley eagerly entered the political race.

The country was fiercely divided over many issues then, especially the war in Vietnam. Shirley believed that Democratic President Lyndon Johnson wasn't paying enough attention to his military advisers. She urged the President to "keep the Communists of North Vietnam from taking over South Vietnam." Shirley had strong opinions about taxes, too. She felt that people paid too much money in taxes and that the government spent too much money, especially on welfare programs that were not effective. At the time, Shirley also spoke out against the President's lack of leadership when it came to "preventing Negro riots."

At her first press conference, Shirley was mobbed by news reporters. Although many people were interested in what she had to say, Shirley had lots of competition. Eleven other candidates were running against her! They represented many different political points of view.

Unfortunately, Shirley could not count on the support of some of her most influential friends. Ronald Reagan and Richard Nixon, for instance, would not be campaigning for her, since both men were busy trying to win the 1968 Presidential nomination.

Shirley's strongest rival was Paul "Pete" McCloskey, a handsome and likable Korean War hero. By the time Shirley entered the race, he'd already gotten a lot of money from his supporters and had hired an experienced campaign manager.

With Charles as her campaign manager, Shirley had lots of love and devotion on her side, but perhaps not as much political know-how. The McCloskey campaign successfully damaged the public's positive view of Shirley by constantly emphasizing her wealth, privilege, and conservative ideas. To some voters, her views seemed harsh.

Shirley made the typical mistakes of someone new to politics, such as refusing to debate her Republican opponents in public. And when she joked about a program to kill rats in poor neighborhoods—where many babies had already been bitten—some voters were outraged.

When McCloskey won the election with 68,920 votes compared to Shirley's 34,521, she was bitterly disappointed. But Shirley's involvement in politics was not over. She would just have to find another way of entering public service—and soon she did.

When Richard Nixon won his party's nomination in 1968, Shirley raised over a million dollars for his campaign by giving more than two hundred speeches nationwide. She even traveled to Europe to organize Americans living abroad to vote.

Then she returned home and spoke on behalf of

Republican candidates for Congress. Always an effective speaker, Shirley gained support for the party, and in the process, she earned the loyalty of many politicians.

In 1969, President Nixon chose her to become a U.S. representative to the United Nations. Both she and Charles moved to New York City, eager to meet this fascinating new challenge.

Ambassador

As a United States diplomat, Shirley Temple Black understood that her first task was to establish a new public image. The memory of "little Miss Temple" had brought much-needed publicity during her Congressional campaign, but now Shirley had serious work to do.

When she arrived at the U.N., other diplomats joked about her, saying "Heidi wouldn't lie." Remarks like this were meant to bring back the image of a curly-headed little girl prancing about the hillsides in wooden shoes, as Shirley had done years earlier in the movie *Heidi*.

But now Shirley attacked her diplomatic job as she had her movie roles—with hard work and a determination to be the best at whatever she was doing. As a result, she was soon accepted as an equal by experienced diplomats.

Shirley served on committees that dealt with many different issues, including education, cultural activities, youth problems, refugees, world peace, and the environment.

The other U.N. delegates couldn't resist asking for her autograph, but they also paid close attention to her speeches. They learned that she was a tough negotiator. When her term came to an end, one delegate publicly announced that Shirley had always carried her "share of the burden and made our work immeasurably easier as an entire delegation."

During the first few months after she left the U.N., Shirley accepted a number of diplomatic assignments. She became deputy head of the American delegation to the U.N. Committee on the Environment. Fighting to make people aware of the dangers facing the environment, she traveled widely in Europe, the Mideast, and the Far East.

For Ronald Reagan, who was then governor of California, she headed the state's efforts to publicize the goals of the United Nations. She also served in Stockholm, Sweden, as the only female U.S. representative to the U.N. Conference on the Human Environment.

In 1974, Gerald Ford, a good friend of the Blacks, became President. President Ford appointed Shirley U.S. Ambassador to Ghana, an important West African country.

Before leaving for Accra, Ghana's capital city, Shirley spent many weeks studying the country's history and learning about the many different languages spoken there. To do a good job, Shirley knew she would have to win the trust of the people as well as the respect of the country's leaders. In addition, she would have to show the embassy staff that she was a hard worker, since many people still thought of her as a child movie star.

Living conditions in Ghana, even for the United States staff members, were not very comfortable. Accra was a beautiful seaside city, but the wind called *harmattan* made it humid and dusty. Malaria, a disease spread by the bite of a mosquito, caused many deaths in the region. The water was full of parasites, so it had to be boiled before it could be used. And snakes and bats moved freely about the grounds of the Blacks' new home!

Nevertheless, Shirley was enchanted. With her usual energy, she worked at the embassy, met with government officials, and traveled all over the country. Observers were amazed by her energy and enthusiasm. She was a popular figure, much admired for her willingness to listen and learn.

Shirley spoke out strongly against the official policies of South Africa, where *apartheid* separated the black and white races. She argued that all African countries should have governments chosen by the majority of the citizens.

Some U.S. diplomats believed that Shirley was too outspoken, as well as abrupt and demanding. They questioned how sensitive she was to the problems of this poor country. But overall, this was a time of great accomplishment for Shirley and her family.

Shirley was proud of her achievements as ambassador and enjoyed the friendship of the Ghanaians. Charles was able to work on his business at their house in Accra, and he spent many happy hours in the pleasant gardens. The Blacks entertained often, and Shirley learned to cook the regional cuisine. Their daughter Susan, now twenty-seven years old, fell in love and married a handsome young Italian diplomat.

Shirley's happy days in Accra would come to a sudden and unexpected end, though, when she unknowingly played a part in an embarrassing incident involving U.S. Secretary of State Henry Kissinger.

In 1976, Mr. Kissinger planned a tour of the African nations. He was not planning to stop in Ghana because he knew its president wouldn't personally welcome his official visit. But when Shirley persuaded the Ghanaian leader to change his mind, Mr. Kissinger agreed to come. Then, on his way to Ghana, Mr. Kissinger learned that the African leader had changed his plans again. Mr. Kissinger would be greeted by minor officials and *not* by the president himself. The American statesman was so insulted that the visit was canceled abruptly.

Shirley lost her job as a result of this incident. When she and Charles boarded the plane for the United States, Shirley had tears in her eyes. Because both countries were angry about the canceled visit, no one was there to say farewell.

President Ford gave Shirley a new job in Washington as chief of protocol. But even though she would have a large staff and the responsibility of arranging many events for foreign heads of state and other important guests of the U.S. government, this new job was politically unimportant.

Shirley was always ready to accept whatever came her way, however, and soon she began to look on the bright side. As the first woman protocol chief, she was determined to demonstrate her organizational talents. Unfortunately, this job didn't last long either because President Ford was not re-elected in 1976. Shirley's last official responsibility in the Ford administration was to plan Jimmy Carter's Presidential inauguration.

This was a sad time in Shirley's life, for personal as well as professional reasons. Her beloved mother died in California just three weeks before the inauguration ceremony. Shirley would always feel that she owed everything to Gertrude's care, confidence, and love. When her father died in 1980, after a long illness, she began to see the importance of telling her own story while she still had a chance. She started *Child Star,* the first volume of her autobiography, which was published in 1988.

Today, Shirley remains active in community, charity, and political organizations. Hollywood remembered her in 1985 with a special Oscar—the correct size this time!

In 1988, she was extremely active in support of George Bush's Presidential campaign. And the following year, she was named ambassador to Czechoslovakia.

There's no telling what Shirley will do next. But whatever it is, she will surely follow Gertrude's advice, as always, and "Sparkle!"

Highlights in the Life of
SHIRLEY TEMPLE BLACK

1928   On April 23, Shirley Temple is born in Santa
Monica, California.

1931   Shirley makes her movie debut in the first
Baby Burlesks film.

1939   Shirley attends the Westlake School for Girls.

1945   Shirley marries John Agar in California on
September 19.

1948   Daughter Linda Susan is born on January 30.

1949   Shirley and John Agar are divorced.
Shirley makes what is probably her last movie,
A Kiss for Corliss.

1950   Shirley marries Charles Black on December 16.

1952   Son Charles, Jr., is born on April 28.

1954   Daughter Lori Alden is born on April 9.

1958   The television program *Shirley Temple's
Storybook* is aired.

1967   Shirley runs for the office of California
congresswoman, but she loses the election.

1969 Shirley is chosen by President Richard M. Nixon to be United States representative to the United Nations.

1974 President Gerald R. Ford appoints Shirley ambassador to the Republic of Ghana. Shirley becomes the first woman to hold the position of United States chief of protocol.

1989 President George Bush appoints Shirley ambassador to Czechoslovakia.

A Shirley Temple *Filmography*

Short Films

The Runt Page (1931)
War Babies (What Price Gloria) (1932)
The Pie Covered Wagon (1932)
Glad Rags to Riches (1932)
The Kid's Last Fight (1932)
Kid in Hollywood (1932)
Pollytix in Washington (1932)
Kid in Africa (1932)
Merrily Yours (1933)
Dora's Dunking Doughnuts (1933)
Pardon My Pups (1933)
Managed Money (1933)
What to Do? (1933)

Feature Films

The Red-Haired Alibi (1932)
Out All Night (1933)
To the Last Man (1933)
Carolina (1933)
Mandalay (1933)
As the Earth Turns (1933)
New Deal Rhythm (1933)
Stand Up and Cheer (1934)
Now I'll Tell (1934)

Change of Heart (1934)

Little Miss Marker (1934)

Baby Take A Bow (1934)

Now and Forever (1934)

Bright Eyes (1934)

The Little Colonel (1934)

Our Little Girl (Heaven's Gate) (1935)

Curly Top (1935)

The Littlest Rebel (1935)

Captain January (1936)

Poor Little Rich Girl (1936)

Dimples (The Bowery Princess) (1936)

Stowaway (1936)

Wee Willie Winkie (1937)

Heidi (1937)

Rebecca and Sunnybrook Farm (1938)

Little Miss Broadway (1938)

Just Around the Corner (1939)

The Little Princess (1939)

Susannah of the Mounties (1939)

The Blue Bird (1939)

Young People (1940)

Kathleen (1941)

Miss Annie Rooney (1942)

Since You Went Away (1943)

I'll Be Seeing You (1944)

Kiss and Tell (1945)

Honeymoon (1946)
The Bachelor and the Baby Soxer (1947)
That Hagen Girl (1947)
Fort Apache (1947)
Adventure in Baltimore (1948)
Mr. Belvedere Goes to College (1948)
The Story of Seabiscuit (1949)
A Kiss for Corliss (1949)

For Further Study

More Books to Read

Child Star: An Autobiography. Shirley Temple
(McGraw-Hill)

Shirley Temple. Jeanine Basinger
(Pyramid Publications)

Shirley Temple: American Princess. Anne Edwards
(William Morrow)

Shirley Temple Black: Actress to Ambassador.
James Haskins (Viking Kestrel)

The Shirley Temple Scrapbook. Loraine Burdick
(Jonathan David Publishers)

The Shirley Temple Story. Lester David (Putnam)

Videos

Shirley Temple Black. (A & E Home Video)
Shirley Temple Scrapbook. (MPI Home Video)

Index

99